R
E
D

S
U
G
A
R

PITT POETRY SERIES

Ed Ochester, Editor

RED SUGAR

JAN BEATTY

UNIVERSITY OF PITTSBURGH PRESS

Published by the University of Pittsburgh Press, Pittsburgh, Pa., 15260

Copyright © 2008, Jan Beatty

Manufactured in the United States of America

Printed on acid-free paper

10 9 8 7 6 5 4 3 2 1

ISBN 13: 978-0-8229-5987-8

ISBN 10: 0-8229-5987-9

CONTENTS

—5 *Red Song*

—6 *Love Poem w/Strat #2*

—7 *after the narrowing, the map*

−1

to the cracked code and the inside job
blood's version of things

I Saw One of Blake's Angels

at the peep show on 10th/singing her
angel song/she was passing through
the ring between heaven & hell/flames
at her feet & men with long fingernails
& grabbing mouths. Beautiful.
She was

transparent with a fire beneath her skin,
her thighs titanic, she was innocence &
experience her mouth the only o in prophesy,
she would fly around the room with her eyes.
My name is Angela, she said, *I can talk when
I'm doing things, what do you want?*
She is

lying back on the pink mohair
pillow/legs spread wide to pink/exposing
the history of Occidental morality with
a small shaved V of wild red/left breast
longer than her right/hanging down like a
nozzle, like rubber/that crazy orangey-
brown/she is

ecstatic in her own longing/18
max/slippery floor/guy down the dark hall
jerking off on the wall/in the fluid stages of
empire & slavery/I like to look at her. I speak
to the phone by the cum-smeared plexiglass/
she is

nearly mythical in her longings, her
boyfriend, new job: *We're getting married
in June/Great,* I say, : *I can play with myself*

if you want/Okay, I say, just like the guardians of
tradition/she passes the glittery pink scarf over
the wild V/pinching her nipples like only
an angel can & giggling: *like this?*
she is

      lifting both feet to the plexiglass/one
inch from my face is her angel-of-blake pussy/
licks her middle finger & shoves it in/working
the only water pump in heaven/screen's sliding/
I'm bending/more quarters
                  & slides &

she is
        singing in a voice to revive
        all the dead:
        is this it?,
                sweet song:
                    is this what you want?

she is
        tracing the pink/of her thighs
        with small pink hands:
        do you like that/
            like that?
          she is the next circle of hell/
         the one where

                  I know
we either stay or go today/no other day/
my face pink in the dark/her dark pink
track lines/we meet in her body/
                together
we roll the dark angel of death/take her
pocket change & prop her

/wedged/
in the dirty corner/we pass the row of lockers/
walk the hallway of swords/the line of hollow-
eyed men/the old woman gatekeeper, wooden
with a face painted gray/
                              we, incandescent
            & bereft/can see the door open/curb

                    of the outside world, our bodies
spinning into the searing white of the afternoon/
after a good night of drugs/we are triumphant
in the downtown litter/
                        I am stunned to find
my own loneliness & magnificence, here/
with her/in my body.

Lip

Edge, verge, labium. Flange, impertinence, recompense.
Road to the mouth inside us, the blue-red slippery,
the not quite in. Insolence, convexity, lip lip
rim. Body collar, curb of the pussy, furbelow, flounce.
Skirt of the known world, threshold to the threshold,
trim. Margin of the valley between thighs, sidle up/
jump. Brink of your first happiness, almost
oops, you're in/edge on.

liplipliplip/bopbopaloobop/as good as dope/almost.
The swoop, the junction, the original front lawn,
one less than a trois, spank it, frisk it, the light goes
on. Sidewise smile, gateway to red. Light summer
jacket & your mama said: save it for a rainy day,
wear a light jacket on a summer night, but she
never rocked the body electric, original e, she
never sang it like that/did your mama? Ever
turn over, drive right up to the window,
say, I'll take some. Give me some spurt, some
rush, some one more time, some honey,
I'm the city, I don't need your map.

-2

Make it Beautiful

> When you tell it, don't say it straight,
> just say:

>> *One dreamy moonlit night she looks up and:*

>>> *the flowers in the curtains are suddenly burning:*

>>> *then say something like:*

>>> *eyes eyes, scream the small o:*

> because no one will believe it, everyone
> is sick of it, and don't ever say:

> *seven years old/tiny pearl/*

> *bramble of hair/thick man/*

slimy girl/spoiled food/

large hands/no door:

,—ever.

Skinning It

What I could never tell was size by looking—
his big enough? Couldn't tell anyone
how the body had become my own set of Legos,
this part into that, in/out, in/out,
I was fucking every man who crossed my path,
random fucking, him or him, no difference, &
I couldn't tell the one about the other—but
not their business & what was the equation:
long slow stride = patient lover, small but smooth?
sideways lean = quick, stop & go fuck?
body builder = small dick, overcompensates?
large hands = large hands, don't count on it.
I wanted ruin/wreckage, the up-against-the-stall-
quick-from-behind-huge-cock-in-me bathroom fuck.
How could I tell my sweetie-sweet friends
that I blew the guy on the rugby team?
on the ferry? in the carport?
or the gargantuan cock of the train
steward, in its rocknroll across
Canada/his cock rolling the train of me?
Why is the raw body so unloved
when it's out-loud? Just veins, blood,
what we're made of? No, it's the greed,
the dying for it I would never tell—
they'd say: she's too hungry, should have
eaten breakfast, man-eater, size queen,
they'd say all that need = I don't want
to know her, all those cocks = slut =
white-trash-train-wreck. Then I'd say, what
are you hiding under your nice-nice-nice?
When's the last time you skinned it hard?
I'd say quiet, polite = not quite
big enough.

I'll Write the Girl

The thing I'll never write is the green leaf
with its rubbery-hard veins, I'll never
write the structure exposed, instead

I'll write the girl picking it up, green leaf,
her pudgy hand & her wanting it, that's it,
because she knows the sky is full

of stumbling ghosts, & she's back in the cold
room, back on the dark floor, & along
so much sky, what does one person do?

She says, *bring it to me* & devours,
hungry girl, breaks it open, tastes
the day's first plasma of leaf, first blood

of green on her city street, she takes it
to her like morning's first kill, &
owns it, stem to point,

& knows her life will always
be this biting open one thing
to leave another, that the only

way she'll get anything is
with this tiny hammer
in her animal brain

saying: *mine,*
& *again,*
& *now.*

Prison Sex

10 am Tuesday you show up at my apt my republican roommates & old italian
neighbors watching. 11 years in jail & I'm your first stop in your too-small suit
& worn shoes you're an East Liberty pimp right to the mattress on the floor
in my no-drapes room & it's you on top of me/suit on/I'm on my stomach in
teeshirt-for-pajamas & we're rolling/slapping/scratching/your hands on my
wrists loud your o deep o like the fucking home-run fuck like your fucking-a-
teenager-first-time fuck & no time for *happy to be out?* shirt up/zipper down &
I'm the guys you fucked in prison/the tearing down they did to you/then breath
that opens the field of bodies inside me waiting to be found/solid evidence of
my sorrows/I had to put them somewhere deep & vast like someone's last long
breath/you're in for murder did you do it/I hear you pushing a wall of breath/
field of air on my back/release/you're out your breath held sharp 11 years
now all that chamber music is mine/some jacked-up fugue all those rooms
of hurt the blistering sins of everyone I never met down my back/fast/you're
ramming me & if I like it who am I/a human? someone as lonely as you?
worse worse whose blood whose air cut short whose once life strangled down
to no life/*do you still love me?* you say/it's out not pretty not real but violet/
colorized/*wait* I say/my hands against the wall at the head of the bed/slam/
I came right over, you say, *was that wrong?*/the prisoner in you asking/*no, no,
I'm glad you're here*/the hostage in me loving the dress laid out/I'm wearing
your body/*release*/the air of your victim dirty & hot is it something I receive?
as what/whose death inside me now? you never said you did it—you come hard
hard not fast living this fuck 11 years/fall into me & cry/I don't know who I am
this half-step pitch of cruelty/slant eye for the shifting lie/I have my souvenirs

To the Well-Meaning

My bazooka fortune: *the highway of fear*
is the road to defeat, so feeling all used up,
I'm writing it down.

I turned my back, forgot
the best part of me, listened to too many people.
Ever think somebody knew you

better than you knew you?
I let you break down the gates.
I was looking for sense & company

in a world of liquid dreams & red sugar.
I'll tell you one thing:
I like getting better than wanting.

I can suck on it, suck & suck it—
Forget the buddhist transcendence thing—
I want it juicy so I can taste it, chew, bleed it.

Bazooka Joe is saying:
Mort is getting on my nerves! He keeps imitating me!
Mort, stop acting like a silly goof!

I thought you wanted to eat life alive/
not pull it out for show. When it's all over, I won't be wishing
for one more conversation to see what you think.

Who do you want at your bedside when you die?
Truthful remorse leads to the fruitful death of the self,
not to its survival as a successful liar.

Iris Murdoch sounds good, but I'm tired
of sweeping the room for another year.
I see now I have a field of 4 to talk to,

& the next sentence should be *lucky lucky lucky.*
Some people say this life is just an idea of a life,
but I say the highway of fear is real.

& so we have this comic, this
poem, this small, small matter of
wanting to eat the world,

swallow it up, say I was here.

Shooter

I shoot the old man who followed my 11-yr-old body on Smithfield St/because
I smiled at him/because it was Xmas/I shoot the man who jacked-off/on
the bricks of our house/put a ladder to my window when I was 12/I shoot the
professor who said my work was illogical, then used me for publicity when I
won an award/the businessman who wanted to talk about my teenage
breasts/I'm loading & re-loading/the guy who walked up to me when I was
a cashier & asked about my "hole"/I hope you still like me when I say the
gynecologist stuck his tongue down my throat when I was 16/the writer who
read his gang rape poem to a room of women students/I'm putting my finger
on the problem/the men who pose as feminists/the predators/the rapists/the
bullies & thugs among us/my uncle who tried to kiss me when he was
drunk/my 60-yr-old neighbor who grabbed me when my parents weren't
home/it was my fault/a man named Roy who wouldn't stop when I said no/he
said *shut up,* he said *now*/he taught me to love the trigger/I'm shooting the
cook who grabbed me from behind in the restaurant kitchen/the famous poet
who said there are no great women writers/the boyfriend who left his handprint
in black & blue/the men who say we're too serious, prettier when we smile/I'm
smiling & shooting/the shrink who tried to lock me up/the boss who gave me a
ride home/wanted a blow job/pushed my head down/the poet who said I didn't
praise him enough/here's one for you/the restaurant manager who told me
to grow a thicker skin & wear a skimpy uniform/because really we have an
attitude/we need to lighten up/I shoot all the men I've left off the list, so I don't
have to worry my pretty little head about it.

Flurry

flurry. morning flurry of the young. boys in green ties. girls in gray

plaid jumpers, running. to catholic school, then the scream. the dash.

race to the glass door. the scream & the dash. race to the glass door of

the foyer. (green tile lobby of the suburban school). girls sprinting full

out to beat the boys. no stopping before the red brick. learning. we

can't beat them. really beat them. but this first year of many. wild

mornings, all of us laughing in bunches. & crowding around him each

day the same. flurry. young children. waiting to be swooped up.

(waiting to be thought of). held too tight, youngness. held too

long, kissed. the patting & hair stroking. I am his favorite. like your

grandfather kisses you. he loves my oblivion. to his hands. he says.

he likes my smile. my 20 years before the charges are brought. my

smallness. priest. stands in his black cassock. next to the list of movies.

we are forbidden to see. by the holy statue. he swings us around. in his

finery. (next to the six ft. thermometer showing how hot). the chart of

the money we raised. how close we are. to our goal. for the christian

children's fund. it was him. there. in the lobby. our gray kneesocks.

our twirling young bodies. touching us.

Red Sugar

You walk inside yourself on roads and ropes
of blood vessels and tendons, you walk inside
yourself and eat weather

Gretel Ehrlich

When I was young, I was a comet
with an unending shimmering tail,
and I flew over the brokenness below
that was my life. I didn't know until I was
twelve that we carry other bodies inside us.
Not babies, but bodies of blood
that speak to us in plutonic languages
of pith and serum. When I was
six, there was a man in the woods,
naked. I didn't know him, but I knew
he was a wrong kind of man/so I ran.
With my inside body I see his skinny
white bones and curled mouth, he looks
like sickness and it's the body inside me
that's running, my red sugar body
that shows me the brutal road to love,
the one good man, the one song
I can keep as mine. I heard it once
when I was waitressing, something
made me turn my head, made me
swivel to look at a woman across
the room, wasn't even my station,
but the red sugar said, *go.* When I
saw her up close, I knew she was
blood. I can't explain this—I only met
my mother once. I said, *Do you know*
a woman named Dorothy? Her face
was pale, she said, *No*—in that hard way.
Maybe her red sugar told her to run—
but before she left, she grabbed my arm,

said, *I did have a sister named Dorothy,*
but she died. Two inches away from her
dyed blond hair, I said, *okay,* but both
our inside bodies knew she was lying.
Some people call it eating weather—
the way you swallow what you know,
but keep it—later it rises like a storm
from another world, reptilian and hungry.
It's the thickness that drives us and
stains us, the not asking/just coming/
the cunt alive and jewel-like/the uncut
garnet and the lava flow/it's barbarism/
bloodletting/the most liquid part of us/
spilling/spreading/the granular red sea
of sap and gore/sinking/moving forward
at the same time/slippery/red
containing blue/it's the sweet,
deep inside of the body.

-3

After Being Fired from the All-Night Greek Diner

the old greek owner said to me:
I bet you're good in bed.
21, I said: *I don't know.*

His head dropped like a coin in a slot:

Look honey, when somebody asks you that,
say, I'm the best. That's all you say,
I'm the best.

The Phenomenology of Sex

I tell my friend Jude
about the phenomenologist I'm dating:

> *We were doing poppers in Texas*
> *in his living room & on our knees*
> *having sex—I turned around to look*
> *just before the big O & saw him*
> *chewing the wooden arm*
> *of the easy chair.*

And then you broke up with him?

> *No. I didn't get the message.*

I tell her how he talks phenomenology to me:
how consciousness is everything, how important it is
to suspend assertions of existence independent of consciousness,
which I take to mean, he's afraid of living.

Jude says:
> *the bottom line is he's chewing*
> *on the chair. What are you gonna do?*

I tell her how, in Pittsburgh, he tried
to teach me how to drive my own car.
How I said to him: *if this car crashed in a forest,*
> *you couldn't hear it, but I would.*

So that was it?

> *Yeah, that was it.*

American Night

I like being scared—but he's
got me in a headlock, shoving my mouth
full with tongue, the car weaving,
I'm thinking, *oh shit.* Ten minutes later
me & 4 guys I don't know
in the Palace Inn men's room
snorting coke off the back of a toilet/
I lift my head/dollar bill in my nose/all of them
looking/*shit I'm in trouble* & grab him,
can't remember his name, *let's go,* figuring
I got a better chance with 1 guy than 5, rub up
against him so he thinks I want him/
we split/coked out of our minds/I say
let's go to my place, hoping he'll be so fucked up
by the time we get there he'll pass out/
we're headed somewhere/
his sister's house he says, I'm grabbing
the mace in my bag/he's big/6 am in
some jacked suburban neighborhood/
can't think/swallowing/just swallowing the high
down the back of my throat, *fuck, fuck*
into this house with shutters/small bedroom
like a young girl's room/twin beds/white frilly
bedclothes/heart spiking its coked-
up rhythm/looking for exits/maybe it is
his sister's house/*c'mere* & pulls me
on top of him in the little-girl bed/I kiss him/
hate myself/say I have to pee & I
leave that room/run into a woman in a fuzzy robe &
glittery green eye shadow in the hall/
she looks at me strange/I want to disappear/disappear & I
find that front door/walk out of it running

In Helena

the bag boy at Albertson's
stared, said, *You like Eminem?*

Knew he meant my shaved blond head,
I said, *Yeah, I like him, do you?*

Oh yeah, &
        dropped his head/
                    quick
          to some cracked
              hip/hop in his head,

the middle-aged cashier
in the '70's smock confused.

It was a burning question, he said.
Then you have to ask it, I said,

& he spun & dipped/
          punched

     the air from the bag's body,
     his green watery
                  eyes our new dangerous sea.
                    He said, *I get off at 9—*

Remembering 18 & dangerous I wanted
to, but said *see ya later/*

              & he popped
        up beside me

so I could hear him breathe:
you don't know what you're missing

I kept walking,
yeah I do, and it's good.

When Foucault Entered the Body

My friend Aaron said he'd like to give Sean Penn
a tongue bath, & I guess that's clear enough,

but I want more. I want to wear men's shoes
because they're stylish, sturdy—& just because

I think Patricia Arquette's beautiful
doesn't mean I want to be her. Just give me a wife

beater & an AK-47 & I'll be Nic Cage
bustin up Con-Air, fuckin A. You can call me

shallow, but in grad school the main theoryhead
called me late at night for advice about his boyfriend

& that's when Foucault entered the body—
give me a break with his "I'm not speaking" routine.

Nobody wants to inhabit his/her own body
all the time—Take my friend Aaron, for example.

When he's irritated, he says, "panties, panties, panties"
& that helps calm him down. & just because

my husband had to explain Popa Chubby, the blues singer,
to me—doesn't mean I'm naïve—just on vacation.

Why stay in the body & miss the ricochet back in,
the cool body return with its jolt of red sugar

& don't you just love the inside out of it?
The veins & pink slippery animal openings of it?

Panties, panties, panties.
When I dress in drag, honey, I'll be in a pink-flower-

prom-gown with a motherfuckin tiara—
because a sharkskin suit would be too much

like home.

The Day I Stripped

down to nothing, his tongue wormy in my throat—it was my first
visit & my gynecologist grabbed my sweetness, said,
Don't tell anyone. His apey arms still covering me, I popped
back outside to my friend Craig in his blue Impala (I didn't have a car) &
I remember what I was wearing, the green & white checkered
girlie shirt (bright, lively) & he said, *How'd it go?*

Fine, I said, & we headed home. 51 south around Maytide &
I had to pee, so we stopped at Joey Carbone's Cocktail Lounge
(really a low-level strip joint) & when I wandered the brown hallways
in my suburban belted coat, one of the girls popped
her head out of a doorway like a bad-ass gidget & said dirty loud:
You the new dancer?

& for a second I was that wild & flexible &
could she see the stripper in me? The doctor's squirmy tongue was still
licking. I wanted to be what she needed & now I was qualified. Something
had happened to her I bet, no one
gets to look so hard so young unless—I said *No,*
I'm looking for the bathroom.
                    Jesus Christ!
            she said, *Where the hell is she?* & popped
            back to her cave.

Years later when they closed & the strippers went down the street
to Stiffy's & their johns or back to being stay-at-home moms, the
workers were stripping the paint from the joint's marquee—& quit one day after half
the name & for 24 magnificent hours, the building existed as "Joey Carbone's Cock"
& not cocktail lounge & it was withered, flaky, but big—
for the first time, as big as he said it was.

Skeet Shooting Out West

Tired of the old questions, whose blood, whose cock,
she goes out among red-tailed hawk for shooting lessons.

Cowboy Doug says: *Here's your shell, inside*
you've got the shot, gunpowder and this here's called a wad.

Shooting her wad from the 20-gauge Winchester,
she imagines her real father (whoever he is) shooting his/

making her. This makes her want a pump-action shot-
gun, something she can relate to. She dearly loves the smell of

gunpowder, is this genetic? Maybe her father was
a cowboy, she's loving the gunmetal/kick in the shoulder/

: lip on the V of her hand aroused, someone's blood
under her skin.

Cave Music—Comet, Montana

Jessie lives in a homemade shack
of tires and stones and car parts.
She rigged a way to catch water
running down the mountain—

I just want to be off the grid, she says.

She's got a master's from NYU and
grey hair that hasn't been cut for years,
almost a full-grown mustache.
She takes me to her studio,
filled with peaceful ocean paintings:

I've been workin on these a while.

James makes models of ghost towns for a living:

I saw the blue orbs again, they
follow me in pictures, I know they're
the manifestation of god, I know
from the time I saved a woman
and her child in the terrible car crash
and the light from the sky showed me
where she was, and I bent the car
door to get to the baby & the blue
fish is everywhere now, alerting
me to my next mission.

When Hendrix heard the cave music, he said:

We plan for our sound to go inside
the soul of the person, actually, and see
if they can awaken some kind of thing

in their mind, cause there are so many
sleeping people.

Last night I walked through town and
the eerie glow of the Gold Nugget Bar
scared me like few things have.
Uranus retrograde for the next 6 months
says the air is unstable and I'm hanging
like a sheet in the wind, feeling lost, the
static when no one is speaking your thoughts.

Out here, they say, don't cross any fences.
20 miles from the Continental Divide,
you can go to the hot springs in Boulder
for primal scream therapy or down into
the radon mines for healing the bones.

Where do you go when the tiny dog has no answer for you?
When the lavender house cannot save you?

Calvin says the radon in the mines
really heals people, he and his friends
emptied a house full of wheelchairs
and crutches after people were cured:

> *If you go into the mines and you're healthy,*
> *you'll get cancer, but if you go in when*
> *you have cancer, the radon will balance it*
> *and rid your body of it. Everybody knows*
> *it's a big government conspiracy*
> *to keep the medical profession going.*

Melinda in the Patriot bookstore was
happy to see me:

It gets so lonely here,
I can have a whole day with no customers.

She showed me her handmade cards,
really lovely, with photographs of wildflowers.
She talked about her husband, how he
got her to join the militia:

> *At first I didn't agree with all of it, but after*
> *I read a few books, I started to see*
> *that we really are being controlled*
> *by the Jews owning the banks and all.*

At the cafe, I love Effie the waitress,
how she lets old Carl stay in the shack
behind the house in return for fixing
things that don't need fixing, her still-
pumped sixty-year-old arms, she
never asks, just pours my coffee, says

> *How ya doin honey,*

I find out she hates her gay son,
disowned him, should I hate her now?

> What song do we want to sing?

When Hendrix closed down Woodstock
with the national anthem, the world became
a better place. Hendrix and his Band of Gypsies—
like he said,

> *We play it the way the air is*
> *in America today.*
> *The air is slightly static, isn't it?*

-4

I woke in the night

we are here alone   alone   nothing
between us and death but one inch

—will we lose each other?
if something was wrong with us

—you said, in love's sweet frame:

it would be like a planet
hitting the sun

don't worry
the deep night

Hitchhike

tulip brightness was nowhere in my family house
because of the red light
that wanted to be red

I left home and started walking

—cold night
stuck my thumb out a mile from home
old guy in his thirties, buick

Where are you going, he says,
I don't care and we are going
to the park, no, not the park—

on the back road, to the field,
now on grass and rocky ground
I'm not scared, pull up to the
big tree/I don't care what it is

this first time in my life
that something could happen
it doesn't matter what he does

he turns the car off, I deliver my mouth,
a package to him, watch his hands on
my leg/his fingers unzip me/

I love the red map of the dash, curve
of the streetlight the many and varied
leaves of the tree I kiss him, and I kiss him
he touches my breast, canceling out
every sentence—

, my mother
is punishing something for existing,
but not me, in this field, under the cover

of his wool jacket/fast, it's faster,
always good to trade one thing for another—

I don't love it but I don't hate it
he smells like beer/the windows fog,
his long hair soft like my sister's
as good as some things/not
as good as others

either way I like this thick place/
/no light just fingers
inside me to the end/fingers inside me
to the end/more than a lot of people get/
knowing that hit/that there, right there/and

bull's-eye/even-without-love there
/no regrets/
I don't need more and
I don't need less, he stops/says:

I can't do this
are you hungry, he says/

as hungry as a person can be—
—*no* I say—he drives to the drive-thru,
what do you want?

I don't care/we eat in the car
why I'm out there at night/
too quiet/my mother's staring

too much/I'm wrong too much/
—the boring weight of that/
again

how old are you/14
you shouldn't be, someone could
—they already have, I say

I'm driving you home/
/take me to that corner

Stray

a guy in a john deere hat tells the reporter: *he was quiet,*
a good neighbor. he took good care of his yard. then we see his body,
sunken in on itself. hair hanging down. feet lurching inches at a time

in shackles. sometimes I look at people and think: *I can feel the blade*
of your little machinery. turning inside you from some generator.
cutting you off from yourself. no trace of the older couple down the street,

their bodies he sliced to bits. up the cement ramp to the county jail,
he looks down. pieces of skin still under his fingernails but nothing
we can see. I think: *look at his undiscovered cities. the buildings rising*

in him and their fierce armies. you can't tell how he packaged them
in 6-inch squares, to be sent through the mail. christmas presents
to the family. now the woman next door: *he made good potato salad.*

brought it to church functions. standing in her yard, she looks down.
imagines his big hands in the dark blades of her grass/sees him cutting
the vegetables next to her daughter in the social hall. newly afraid,

she looks out into the camera: *this is a good neighborhood. nothing*
like this ever happens here. if someone strays from themselves,
does it turn the good in them to dust? here's what I know: we don't want

any trouble. what if he was split off from all kindness from the beginning?
I think: *you are all little frankensteins: all little broken-down machines.*
you put your head down. one foot in front of the other. lurching.

The Long White

I think it was a Lincoln, the man's hand
coming from the open door: *c'mere,*
in front of my house, I was 9, I stood still.
I want to talk to you. I started walking
toward school the long white beside me
and I wasn't really scared—just in another
separate place of my own, I wasn't wishing
for anything, just watching my feet walking fast,
the hand reaching out, could they see
a fresh girl who didn't know
her real parents: the wide-open face
with no protection, the paleness that says,
I'm lonely, I'm wandering and could be
scooped up in a minute if you insist—
I just want to talk to you,
and after a while I just jumped in.
I thought of this twenty years later when
the cab pulled up and there was fog and
three ravens sitting on the wooden totem of
the ashes of dead Inuit, I stepped into
the long white outside the closed train station,
5 am Prince Rupert, British Columbia
the cab pulled up, the same man's hand
threw open the passenger door, the same
question: *need a ride?*
Yes, yes, I climbed in
but this time I told about it:
blurted my story to this stranger, a father
who I never knew, never knew where
he was from, someone said a hockey player
from Canada and he said *yes, yes,* and I told him
I always wondered about my father,

and his head swung around and he insisted:
you need to look for him, you need to do this,
I didn't know I had been getting in cars
with men all my life looking for him,
a passenger in the long white, until then.

The Arrangements

Aunt Charlotte made arrangements
20 years before she died:

she supplied:

> *white underclothes*
> *lacy white camisole*
> *ankle socks*
> *a pearl ring she bought*
> *for $13 at a hospital gift shop*
> *(she had money, wasn't cheap,*
> *but she liked the ring and laughed*
> *when people complimented her on it)*

> *the pink negligee she picked out with*
> *her sisters 20 years before (they sat*
> *at the kitchen table discussing*
> *their respective colors)*
> *a small crucifix to be placed*
> *in the casket, a black beaded wooden rosary*
> *to be placed in her hands (it once belonged*
> *to aunt rosella, who was a nun)*

> *get the letter of instructions from bonnie, she said*
> *it's all written down*

On that day, the instructions were followed.
We chose pink and white lilies, white irises
and white spider mums:

what the world gave her:

st. george's cemetery
on a beautiful warm day—
10 drops of rain as we huddled
in the cement block chapel with dirty
yellow curtains and piles of flies
in the windowwells

the priest used the time to
talk about being a proud American
during during this Iraq war, joke
about his golf score, lecture us
on how grateful we should be,
warn us of our mortality

In that bunker I prayed for him
to be struck dead, to be wrapped in dirty
yellow curtains, to be devoured by flies.

Luck Was the Father

Something has to give for me to keep sane.
Someone has to make way for nothing.

Brian Palmer

At 10, I sewed two pillowcases together
to climb into at night, save me
from the cars pulling up, the man coming
to the window—I wanted to be ready.
Afraid to take a shower in case the man
with the knife—I picked up the cracking
hammer to finish the job of me, but my father
stopped me—not him, but the thought
of him. I would have been buried by
my dark ideas, a natural path to falling:
I was never watery or moody—
I chose the straight-ahead plan,
plotting year after year
to kill myself, pain so sharp I just
wanted it over—at the end,
who would find me? I couldn't stand
my father seeing the mess of me,
knowing he would hurt and hurt,
so luck for me was the father I had—
he knew somehow I needed
a place to be, he made a bunker for me:
40 x 40 plywood, a platform he built
in the attic, where I kept myself
with books he bought—a lamp,
some food, and a trap door closed
behind me in the blue light.

Long White Sky

It was something about the long white sky,
the open highway feeling of no stops
that flooded me when I was washing her hair.
She had never let me touch her, never
hugged much, so when I had my hands
in her thin brown hair, careful not to hurt,
I found myself in the inner sanctum
of the body in the way that only happens
when someone allows you to assist.

What did I know of her daily scars?
here, tender,

> *where you fell on the stairs. here,*
> *where the priest patted your head*
> *at first communion. here where*
> *your brother hit you?*

This head covered by so many hats
in your 94 years, now my hands
on your scalp, rinsing water through—
knowing I can't retrieve you,
you have let me near:

I will never hurt you, never pull or
overstep—I'm in love with finding
what you need, can I help, really
in the smallest way:

> *here/no/ not*
> *there/ too much/*
> > *wait—*

Standing with you in the long white,
handmaiden as you ready your body

into next sky:
　　　　you lie back,
　　　　inch your body deeper in the hospital bed
　　　　arms at your sides,
　　　　you pat the sheets smooth,
　　　　then hands crossed over your
　　　　blue nightgown, and yes.

Speculator Mine Disaster   Butte, Montana, 1917

The light was waning and I wrote my letter

James D. Moore

the body
remembers the telephone line
    June 8, 1917
the slant light   the alley behind
    Dear Pet,
the shack/the hole
    This may be the last message from me.

and the colors of the place
    The gas broke about 11:15 pm.
(copper light)
    I tried to get all the men out,
rusted crane at the base
    but the smoke was too strong.
of the neighbor's hill
    I got some of the boys with me in a drift

dear dust frosted over
    and put in a bulkhead . . . if anything

dear side door sticking
    happens to me you had better sell the house . . .

the body remembers sea level
    and go to California and live.
as the colors are dying,
    You will know your Jim died like a man

the body takes itself there
>*and his last thought was for his wife*

and writes a letter:
>*that I love better than anyone on earth. . .*
dear old mine bucket   rock   rails,
>*We will meet again.*

to the red blood waters of the mine
>*Tell mother and the boys goodbye.*
waste   bodies lost
>*With love to my pet*
dear underground fires,
>*and may God take care of you.*
there.

Procession

Little wren, your body is breaking down into air.
I find you under my desk,
—how long dead?—
What do the hollowed black cones of your eyes
and your tiny claws have to tell me about home?
Your small patch of city yard,
droop of telephone wire on your daily flight,
the wind draft over the Allegheny?

I pray to the four directions
then put your body in the trash, cover you
with typewriter ribbons and calendar days and press down.
Ten minutes later I dig you out,
carry you outside in the styrofoam box
and we walk the streets of Etna
while big-haired women watch from their porches.

Across Butler Street,
the workers of the Tippins Machinery Plant
break open their lunch buckets on the stone wall.
At the churchyard I dig behind the hydrangea
with my father's tack-hammer and cast-iron awl.
Everything goes on without us.

If I could see the cities inside you,
if I could find my own ocean of light—

In the hole:
paper with a stamp of an orange sun on it
and the word: /FINISHED/
a piece of carnelian and last words:
I am sorry. I know you were alone in this room of poems.
I tried to hide your death.
RIP May 29th Calvert United Presbyterian Church.

5

Red Song

There's a great river running under me
a red song for the babies
bloody turnips on the infant tree
I'm tired of the ruin
and the artichokes with their fibrous heads
and I could say distantly: *the aisles of the world*
are glutted with blood and rutabagas,
and *see the entrails of birds hanging*
from the clotheslines of the rich and despondent,
and that would sound like Neruda
but not nearly as good, and I'm not caring—
just this: they were moving in me
       there were three

Serum

It is another of the old alchemical truths that
'no solution should be made except in its own blood.'

Nor Hall

I was afraid I had changed. I felt like table salt instead of the red tomato,
the thin reed at the side of the water & not the water. In night dreams
no longer was I chasing the bad man through the dark woods &
stabbing him—now I was in a world of wood & glass—
the insides of the world were missing—I was a passenger
riding up & down grey streets & there were no fires.
I wanted to be the red sugar of the pomegranate—open me up & all
my beautiful seeds there for you.

I encountered the dead & they seemed to have more power in an
offhand turn of the head than I did in my distant stare.

You could say I was meeting my own death in the dream, blah, blah.
I'm telling you my dreams used to be liquid, morphy & cinematic—you
could feel the blood (red sugar) when you were shot—it was swampy, savage,
real & surreal, fleshy & red.—it was hemorrhage & blight, but in a good way.

X   X   X

In the hospital they lifted my uterus like a suitcase
of knobs & tubers, threw it in a haz/mat bin.

Forget what you know about orderly living rooms,
there were tumors against the breakwall,
no channel to light.

I was lost in anesthesia between
the red sugar night & the golden
city of waking.

In the history of my uterus, there has been only one area rug.
the bordering couch, bordering plant, the framed frame.

I used to believe:
        there are long red corridors & polished
wooden floors in the rooms of your uterus,

in the uterus of *her* & *her,* that *she* & *she*
        get up in the morning & notice the trees
        & the reflection of light on the lake is stunningly
        calming for the *she's* & the stillness isn't death but another
        kind of life:

        I was wrong.

                X   X   X

In the hospital/

        I can't think my supernatural thoughts/
leap tall buildings/can't put together a sentence/can't
speak it—& you know that's everything—

        I see my beautiful husband's
face & can't reach for him—

I wonder about the dying, how people confess their sins to them
as a courageous act/the whole time the dying person thinking:
        get this person out of here

                X   X   X

                What would you bring back from the surgeon's table?

Don't bore me with what you've read—

        your latest frozen sea, your house on fire—
        I've got my hands full right here.

        I want to know what the blood knows
        how the red sugar says: stay or go/

how to snap back my wrist/
like a switchblade/
how to know if ten years from now the people I love will turn
into someone else, if all this living is worth it/how to jack ahead/
& get to the sweet pulp of it/stop thinking I don't know
what I know, how to read the tea leaves;

what my birth father's life was like/why he won't claim
me, I want lineage, serum, all the thick gooey answers:
stock & strain; pedigree;
—I said,
take everything out—all my insides—
they don't relate to anything anyway;

X X X

Days before my father died, I went to set the record straight/
crazy idea/him waving his hand in front of me saying/
it's not important/it's not important—then,
I think I know who you are by now—the most beautiful
words for me, words so sheer I slid my hands right through them.
When light left & the big wall came,
I was in my apartment, walking my own brutal planet
of knives & tightropes without a plan for love.

When I got to the hospital/I saw his body/so empty
without him/
& it was no outer space adventure/
nothing mystical: one hand
on the door, then gone

X X X

& my body now, coming apart—

think storeroom & honeycomb,
studio apartment, tastefully decorated:

Look, I'm building a house
from scratch, don't talk to me
about family, about sweet—

*family history, anyone
in your family have cancer?*

I slashed the surgeon's form
with a rough X—scrawled: ADOPTED
across it in 4-inch letters—

I said, *Take everything out*

> not *holymarymotherofgod
> blahblah at the hour
> of our uterus, teach me how
> to love if I can't be a mother
> oh god oh blah precious mother*

X   X   X

Some days the world demands a dress of me—

something to parade around in—

& some days I do too:

> inside out, I'm stitched with hair/
> beaded with eyes/all my seeds
> arranged for you/
>
> but lately since I died inside—
> (fuck the bloody show)
> I'll keep my body mine.

~~*Postscript to the babies that never were:~~
~~I carry your outline on the inside of my eye-~~
~~lids, I carry your blood in my eye~~

X   X   X

Outside is nothing, nothing, nothing. I will construct
three leaning crosses for my uterus:
one for the useless waiting boat,
one for the promised city with its shimmering lake,
one for everything that's not coming.
Then I'll burn it all down.

X   X   X

Procreate this:

Who is the woman after flight?

she's the night/

coming into view:

X   X   X

A Necessary Waist: Plath Grows Thinner Reading Stein

> *. . . what is the current that presents a long line*
> *and a necessary waist*
>
> Gertrude Stein

1. The outside pressing in like a red lake,

causing a narrowing of her.

Will there be room for everything/everyone inside?

2. Because also inside her: a rope and a map:

rope of intestines, marking the equator of her

like the belt of a shirtwaist dress,

map of her mother's face,

every line and malignant flap of skin.

3.   A recording like a tapeworm: *do not return to this*

and

this is everything, everything

you don't want to be.

6

Love Poem w/Strat #2

it's a cross/
    between/
  a greek lyre and
    a peach
        cadillac
        /it

            /rings/
   like a bell when/
       you play it right—

   my baby

plays the/
   lightweight/
       spring=tension

    tremolo bar at the bridge/
             we hit

     the sweet
      notes
      all
      night

A Vegas Thing

She loves the circus of it/like her life/the spinning
wheel of fathers & mothers/who could it be?

She hits the Hard Rock, pulls the guitar handle
of the Hendrix-are-you-experienced? slots. Hell, yeah,

she thinks, & knows Jimi is her real father since
she was born on his birthday, day of electrifying excitement

it says in the astrology books. She loves rootless
Vegas, her mothers the hookers with hard tans, the white-

trash easterners with full clevelands (white shirt/
white shoes) are definitely her fathers, their bellies &

ties jiggling seductively—she's waiting to be
electrified/sits on the lap of the first leather-y guy she can

find/eats some guitar-shaped waffles with him after
sex/looks better than he fucks/fucks like he's ½ asleep/

could be the heroin/but she was looking for hard
rock/a vegas thing.

After

The day after our first date(fucking in the car)
I was trying out phone sex, said, *Tell me what you're wearing.*

Pink taffeta, you said. Second date, snorting coke
at the Castle of Blood, my 3rd shot of ouzo thinking *this*

is my moment, lights low in the after-hours club,
like my mother told me it would be:

hit it hard before the drugs wear off, & I
proposed at the bar in my texas spike boots & day/

old jeans, staring at the dirty red wallpaper &
you said in your best McKees-Rocks-take-no-prisoners

way: *let's get outta here.* & like stone pilgrims
or born-agains we stepped into the searing light of the

5 am Bloomfield street, it happened like I saw it
in the storm sky 20 years ago:

riding off with my man into the rocked-out galaxy.

Dreaming Door

FOR DON

You brought donuts in the morning of our first days and
we watched the great rivers through my South Side windows/everything
swelling, we ate in the turquoise kitchen and opened the dreaming door:
our Pittsburgh rolling by on the coal barges, the P&LE carting steel
to the still-rising cities of the West, a couple speedboats
running the dirty summer Monongahela,
you on your way to work. I said *no one's ever*
been this nice to me as I walked you the 52 steps down
from my third-floor apartment, you tilted your head,
looking at me in a way I'd never seen:
like I was the most sublime person,
your blue eyes seeming truly puzzled:
I haven't even started to love you yet,
and at the door the world barreling through—
this time with gifts, fierce fires,
and planets of luck.

The Punch

My father at thirty
knows the bend over & take it,
but he also knows the flipped switch,
the moment of recalcitrance, when the burn
turns to fire, when the body's magma rises
up, comes out the mouth in a full-blown

motherfucker, when the fist swings high
in its 60-degree orbit to an uppercut.
130 lbs, all frame, he knows the full 90
into a roundhouse slam, then the walking
away, not broken, but changed.
My father's geometry is one body

up against the wall with trouble
on your hands, but less trouble than
if you turned your back, & sometimes
anger is the only right language.
His punches swing clean like a pendulum
into his boss's big-knob head & barrel-chest:

Beatty, get over here and re-do this,
you really fucked this up—
& my father knows he did a fine job,
that this is the language of breaking a man down
until he doesn't fight anymore, because
my father is mouthy, he's union,

Steelworkers Local #1272,
he has opinions about hours & working conditions,
the air they're breathing. When his boss
calls him out, his head lifts to a glare—

he walks slowly over & delivers an uppercut
to the jaw, with a trajectory that leads

from ground to body in a geometry so sweet
you can figure distance, velocity, & angle
to conjure the exact position of the bodies
when the blows are struck, ciphering
through mathematical model the reason
2 grown men/bodies 10 inches apart/

round their fists up & swing a parabola
from this cement floor to this corrugated wall/
figuring in the percentages: rage infused
by union-management history/x the cost
of one man's life in this rust town,
city of steelworkers who built the country/

adding: 2 daughters/the price of 1 man's
dignity & a life of work—1 roundhouse
punch/the backswing casting off blood
in a spatter on the wall of the mill, decking
the boss in a circle of steelworkers cheering:
red on grey a siren bleating: /violation/

so that the investigator will find
an overlay on the corrugated steel:
blood, spatter over spatter.

Love Poem w/Strat

My baby's got a solid-body
guitar, rocks it hard like dinosaurs
eating cars, plays it dirty like worlds
exploding, like Stevie Ray's battered strat,
Badlands sticker on the back, he's got a fever
for the steamroller, like Hendrix on Voodoo Child,
like Jeff Beck avalanching notes into air/
my baby's a gunslinger, plays
his guitar rock-hard—
he likes it old-style, he likes it Muddy,
likes it Elmore James, bends it crazy
on his '62 reissue arctic white strat
& his head rolls back/
to that precise pain, that one note screaming,
his mouth twisted open & the light crossing
his face like a freight train passing—
my baby's a gunslinger, plays
his guitar rock-hard—
he likes it Freddie King/whole body vibrato/
likes it Howlin Wolf, my baby plays it
strings-against-the-mic-stand dirty/twists
the body to the Hubert Sumlin script/screams
through his Fender vibro-king—he's
got a hard-on for traditional, fuck
special effects, fuck overplay/he's got love
for his whammy bar, got love
for his double cutaway fins, jams
his headstock into the air, rips a hole
in the sky with his song

-7

after the narrowing, the map
& the rope,
          I cross the red lake
                    into view

Daughter of Blue Lake

Before I was born, I was a star
over Blue Lake, I was alive before
I was alive, hanging over Blue Lake
in the most romantic of ways—
I stayed until my name was called
and lived today—

        —my place now here,
sitting at your hospital bed watching
you die, I'm reading *Swimming to Antarctica,*
feeling that's how impossible it is
to lose you and waiting for the morphine
to take you and the sky carry you,
not knowing if you can hear,
telling everything I ever wanted
you to know:

Thank you for naming me, I say.
(When my parents picked me out
you told them what to call me)
I like my name, I say, and with eyes
closed you say, *You're welcome.*
I named you before you were born—

    and I'm stroking your hand as
    whatever holds things together
    lets loose, and beyond the field
    of this moment, we fly—

    I see you back then: gatekeeper
    of the other world, saying,
    here, this way, here she is,
    delivering me from the shimmering

to the turbulence of the known world,
    saying: *protect her, care for her*

In the hospital bed,
you never open your eyes
and in the body letting go, you usher me again
to this washing and grooming where
the waves and fault lines of the day take over—
this way/   over here/no matter—
you are flying to your own open book,
your dead brother waiting for you in the car.

Shower w/notebook

I'm dreaming Akhmatova carving holy words
into soap—

              poems in my head in the shower
where I get my dazzling ideas,

             I'm washing myself sweet
for my lover while my mind's craving
sounds & lines—

                    I carried
        The Cost of Discipleship by Reinhold Neibhur
        & a copy of *Good News for Modern Man,*
        I wanted to burn the physical
              down to a new shape,
           leave the world, scar my face like St. Theresa's
for that searing higher purpose/

           I'm asking Rukeyser,

           who was split in half/
           single mother,
           |intercepted|

                   she knew, she recorded:
                   the prolonged wound consciousness
                   after the bullet's shot

              then gave her body
        to politics/recording the senate hearings
        of the white man's sins:

                 What am I retrieving?

              my feet in the porcelain pool,
                 my thighs lathered & touching,

& still I can't understand the body/

I'm half lover dreaming up schemes
to please me/half fighter
      warring the wicked world:

Aphrodite's here/my brain on fire
      & I'm sketching figure 8's:

      see me circle each breast
      with my finger,
      over/under   always coming
       to the same place:

why is it some of us land in the killing zone?
where the wish we can't make, the thing
     we can't get to is all there is?

      —if you say I'm argumentative,
resistant—I say I'm giving you a love poem of
30 years of hard living & bad road &

      my thighs are almost ready for you, smooth
      & frothy, see how the water
      splits the east & west of me

    I learned from
Plath & Sexton   it was breath/taking:

    Stars and showers of gold—conceptions! conceptions!
    I remember a white, cold wing . . .

            here is the jewel,
      here is the excitement the nipple learns

then Olds burned words in my body
in this weather
of steam & rivulet:

in her loose shirt her breasts like white wolves' heads
sway and snarl

Too much body   .

confessing, they said,

& swept you away—

Today I write:
I first learned war in my own body/
happy to bleed my way into bed with the first,
happy to bleed my way to the next, I did it
because I wanted it—for the biting joy of it

because we've all been loved & demolished & if you
haven't, well,
the man on the street might be table scraps to you—

maybe you died young & kept on living—
there's not much I can say except maybe
hard against the wall is *what is.*

2006 I'm a woman writing poems:
cut the blue cord
wipe the last blood
(we're still being washed away)

Sitting Nude

The torso facing east, the head nearly west,
as if she couldn't take in the sight of her
own skin and its failings, its parts spilling
onto other parts. She thought:
Nothing for once.
Too tired for fantasy.
If a body can be seen as itself and loved,
it's a wonderful thing. If the thing-ness
of the body is all, we're doomed and
broke apart: *I'm offering you my breasts,*
inches below the fuselage of my heart,
for whatever a short life can become.

"Lip" is for Tamara DiPalma.

"Make it Beautiful" is for Bruce Weigl.

"To the Well-Meaning" makes use of some lines from *The Good Apprentice* by Iris Murdoch.

"Red Sugar" makes use of some phrases from *A Match to the Heart* by Gretel Ehrlich.

"The Phenomenology of Sex" is dedicated to Judith Vollmer.

"When Foucault Entered the Body" is for Aaron Smith.

"Cave Music" makes use of some lines from an interview with Jimi Hendrix on *The Dick Cavett Show,* and from *Crosstown Traffic,* Charles Shaar Murray, 1998.

"Speculator Mine Disaster   Butte, Montana, 1917" makes use of lines from a letter by James D. Moore that appears on the Speculator Mine Memorial, Butte Montana. The Granite Mountain–Speculator Mine fire on June 8, 1917, remains the country's worst hard-rock, metal mining disaster. The memorial was dedicated in 1996, in honor of at least 167 men who perished, and all the miners in the Butte area.

"Love Poem w/Strat #2" and "Love Poem w/Strat" make use of lines from "The Stratocaster," an article by David Fricke, in which he quotes guitarists Jeff Beck and Joe Perry, *Rolling Stone* 922, May 15, 2003.

"After" is for Don.

"The Punch" is for Robert T. Beatty, who worked for J& L Steel in Pittsburgh, Steelworkers Local #1272, Southside Works.

"Daughter of Blue Lake" is in memory of Charlotte Thoma.

"Shower w/notebook" is after a poem by Judith Vollmer, "Self-Portrait with Notebook" from *The Door Open to the Fire.* It makes use of a few phrases from the following: *Collected Poems* by Muriel Rukeyser; *Selected Poems* by Sylvia Plath; *Complete Poems* by Anne Sexton; *Satan Says* by Sharon Olds.

ACKNOWLEDGMENTS

The author wishes to acknowledge the following journals in which some of these poems first appeared: *Chautauqua Literary Journal* ("Long White Sky," "Procession"); *Cimarron Review* ("The Long White"); *Court Green* ("A Necessary Waist: Plath Grows Thinner Reading Stein," "The Phenomenology of Sex," "Red Song,"); *5 AM* ("The Day I Stripped," "I Saw One of Blake's Angels," "Prison Sex," "The Punch," "Skinning It,"); *Florida Review* ("I'll Write the Girl"); *Gulf Coast* ("Red Sugar," "Stray"); *Heartlands* ("The Arrangements," "Daughter of Blue Lake,"); *Indiana Review* ("When Foucault Entered the Body"); *Paper Street* ("Sitting Nude"); *Pearl* ("Make It Beautiful," "Skeet Shooting Out West"); *Quarterly West* ("Lip").

"Dreaming Door" first appeared, and "Procession" and "The Long White" are reprinted in, *Artifice and Marrow: Contemporary Poems by American Women,* edited by Andrea Hollander Budy.

"Flurry" first appeared in *After the Bell: Contemporary American Prose about School,* edited by Maggie Anderson and David Hassler.

I would like to express my appreciation to the Pennsylvania Council on the Arts; the Pittsburgh Cultural Trust and the Howard Heinz Endowment and Laurel Foundation; the Creative Capital Foundation; Ucross Foundation, Clearmont, Wyoming; Montana Arts Refuge, Basin, Montana; the Jentel Foundation, Banner, Wyoming; and the Ragdale Foundation, Lake Forest, Illinois, for fellowships and support that helped me to write these poems. Special thanks to the Fondazione Lucio Fontana in Milan for the gracious use of the work of Lucio Fontana; thanks to the Carnegie Museum of Art for their assistance; particular thanks to Lulu Lippincott and Marilyn Russell for continued support. I would also like to thank the following people who have helped me with these poems: Nancy Krygowski and Lois Williams for chocolate & lounging at Bartlett Street; Toi Derricotte, Kristin Naca, and Yona Harvey for helpful comments; Peter Oresick, Stefan Lovasic, and Terrance Hayes for impromptu workshops; thanks to Joan Bauer for community and California poetry; Joseph Karasek for spirit and afternoon walks; Jean Valentine for kindness and friendship; Anita Byerly for her enduring poems and good heart; Leslie McIlroy for her beautiful book and brave living; Silas for red paintings; special thanks to Maggie Anderson for years of friendship and generous help with these poems; Irene McKinney for courage and saying it straight; RJ for poem insight; Aaron Smith for line breaks, the best dirty talk, and marathon poetry sessions; Judith Vollmer for poetry feasts, ports of entry, and cosmic dream messages that shaped this manuscript; Ed Ochester for treasured guidance, good humor, patience, keeping me on the road; thanks to my students for their wild spirits; Kayla Sargeson, my favorite intern; Amy Sutton for strawberries and busting loose; Max King for integrity and support; Janice Burley Wilson and the women at *She Said;* Romella Kitchens for her brave work; Don Rosenzweig for poetis interruptus and mud pie; the WYEP gang; Joseph Wilk for being one of a kind; Laurin Wolf for spooky poems and for being herself; Brian Siewiorek for his hair and going for it; Ellen Wadey, partner and friend who has my back in a bar fight; Brent Wadey for best tattoos and unstoppable spirit; Michael Wurster, reigning poetry hero; Ann Townsend, action-figure designer; Gerry LaFemina, clown baby; Joanne Samraney for continuing; John Belch for great heart and taking the leap; Sharon Dynak of Ucross for Wild West help; David Romtvedt for generosity; Michael Simms for loving poetry; Ann Tomer for X-rated quiltmaking; Dyke Action Machine for dyke action; Sandy Yanone for red sugar; Ellen Smith for her honesty and fine poems; Bruce Weigl, Gary Copeland Lilley, Patricia Smith, Sonia Sanchez for inspiration; Bryher for kindness and seeing things; Regin and Linda the chef at Ragdale for great heart; Lynn at Jentel for her boots and jeans; Stacey Waite for speaking it; Granite for vision and bravery; Sankar Roy for perseverance; Jay Carson for his "rat" poem; Richard St. John for constancy; Rina Ferrarelli for expert, timely translation; Guerilla Girls for saying it loud; Christina Murdock for narcoleptic mother poems (and fashion); Bernadette Ulsamer for bra poems (and fashion); Allison Adelle Hedge Coke, sister, for unbridled courage; Tu Fu for *Night Thoughts While Traveling* and *Serum;* Justin Vicari for prevailing; Leone Paradise, an original; Kay Comini for her romantic ways; Britt Horner for Spring Church Book help and fun stories; (cheers for Quincy); Lori Wilson for writing quiet poems that aren't quiet; Dr. G for getting it; Lois Greenberg for going for it; Bobby at the rock shop for believing in it all; Tess Barry, cosmic sister (uncensored) and Thom for exuberance, poetry, and football; Bobby Marchese, mayor of Highland Park; Jimmy Cvetic, Secret Society of Dog; Alan Cadwallader for front-lawn stories; Mike Sweeney for wild paintings; my friend Paul; Bounce for jokes and reinvention; Gary Hollowood for car support; Gerry Rosella Boccella, explorer; Susan Sailer for going after it; Colleen K. for opening the world; Ruth Hendricks for jumping in; Louise Sciannameo for showing how it's done; Gayle Reed for being Gayle Reed; Jo Ann Pratt for her irrepressible self; Bill and Jean for travel support and PI work; Michael McColly for great humanity; Tamara DiPalma (et) for emotional availability and under-the-gun design; Mad Dog (you ain't no hamburger) Brooks for wild barking; Marla for cosmic haircuts; Stacie Amatangelo-Warneke, soul sister, for knowing the real story; Ann Begler for giving room; Laurie Graham for *Singing the City;* Vera Hollowood for Sagittarian bluntness and love; Helen Lorenz for waitress stories; Betty Primm for doing it her way; Barbara D. for the chocolate cake; Dorothy Holley, treasured friend, for poems of zest and joy; Tom and Barb for loving us anyway; Jay Flory for his singular mojo; Katie Hogan, rock star; Rhoda for being who she said she was; Lynn Emanuel for years of support; Ellie Wymard for kind help; Evelyn Pierce for Mississippiness; the

Carlow gang, especially Lou Boyle, for opening the door; Roberta Foizey/forearm club; Rebecca for the RED ROAD; Beth from Minnesota for outside information; Ken Steinken for loving the West; remembering Bailey; Pat Bernarding for still being there; all the Madwomen for their far-ranging talent, resilience, stubbornness, tenderness, and madness—and Patricia Dobler for her guiding spirit that continues; remembering Mary Agnes Capozzoli for her poetry and uncontainable self; remembering Sekou Sundiata, Jack Wolford, John Toth, R. T. Beatty, and Big Jim Hollowood; Charlotte Thoma who saw beneath it all; and Don, who makes it all worth doing.